THE
TESTAMENT
OF
SAMSON

A Chronicle of Strength, Betrayal, and Redemption

As Received By
Dennis Logan
The Honorable Scribe

THE TESTAMENT OF SOLOMON

First Edition.
Published by Penemue Media LLC
Richmond, Virginia, USA

ISBN: 978-1-964297-12-5

This edition of *The Testament of Solomon* is a modern literary and philosophical presentation inspired by ancient pseudepigraphal traditions. Names, characters, entities, and events are rendered symbolically, mythologically, and allegorically. Any resemblance to actual persons, living or dead, is coincidental and serves a creative, theological, or scholarly interpretive purpose.

Library of Congress Control Number: Pending
Printed and bound in the United States of America.

Publisher's Note:
This work is presented as a hybrid of scholarship, visionary literature, and mythopoetic reconstruction. While grounded in the biblical cycle surrounding Samson and the Judges of Israel, this edition is not intended as a ritual manual or doctrinal guide. Rather, it is offered for contemplative reading, literary reflection, and exploration of the symbolic legacy of Samson as a figure of covenant, strength, downfall, and redemption.

Dedication

For she who taught me the cost of trusting love unguarded—
I have laid down my anger and named it peace.
You move as the world made you,
and I forgive that.

And to the four souls born of that storm,
you are the breath that steadied my hands,
the living proof that strength need not be rage.

*"O Lord, remember me, I pray Thee,
and strengthen me only this once."*
— *The Book of Judges 16:28*

Preface

They told me the story was legend—half myth, half sermon,
a moral fable preserved through memory's smoke.
But I have learned that the line between scripture and
secret history
is drawn not by truth,
but by who dares to remember it aloud.

What follows is not invention.
It is translation.

In 2023, during my research for *The Universal Bible* recordings,
I was invited to examine a collection of Coptic and
Syriac fragments
held by a private antiquities conservator in Luxor.
Among the cataloged items was a bundle of vellum leaves
sealed in a clay cylinder, unearthed during drainage work
near the ruins traditionally identified as
Gaza's ancient fortress quarter.
The jar bore no royal seal,
only a faded impression of two pillars joined by a line of script:
"Zorah remembers."

Most dismissed it as a pious forgery,
a monastic invention from the early Christian centuries—
perhaps another apocryphon designed to moralize Samson's fall.
But one passage caught my eye:
a notation written in a steady but untrained Hebrew hand—
not priestly, but personal.
It began:
"I came at dawn with a clay cup and a roll of skins..."

That single sentence changed everything.

The fragments were brittle and smoke-darkened,
written in a dialect mixing late Hebrew with early Aramaic
inflection.
Their tone was unlike any canonical account—
intimate, weary, filled with the cadence of witness.
This was not a prophet speaking in symbols,
nor a priest interpreting myth.
This was a friend recording a confession.

Over several months I compared the fragments
with Samaritan and Qumran materials.
The ink composition and fibers aligned roughly with the 10th
century BCE strata—
consistent with early Iron Age preservation.
More striking was the diction:
certain idioms appear only in the borderland speech
between the Philistine coast and the Danite hills—
a linguistic fingerprint placing the writer exactly
where the Book of Judges situates Samson's final days.

Whoever this scribe was, he was real.
And he was there.

Scholars will debate authenticity as they always do.
Some will say it is a late allegory,
others a poetic invention born of captivity tales.
But I am not a scholar. I am a listener.
And what I heard in these pages was not mythology—
it was memory trembling through time.

As I read, I felt the tone of confession give way to revelation:
the great judge of Israel no longer boasting of strength,
but reckoning with its cost.
This was not the Samson of children's stories or pulpits,
but a man stripped of triumph,
speaking softly into the dark before his final act.

I have rendered the text faithfully,
preserving the scribe's shifts between prose and lament,
between witness and worship.
Where the originals were damaged,
I have supplied connective sense, not invention.
The rhythm you will hear—the weight between pauses—
is drawn from the text itself,
as though it were meant to be recited more than read.

The work you now hold is thus not mere translation,
but resurrection:
the *Testament of Samson,*
as told by the Scribe of Zorah and restored through my hand.

It is, I believe, the oldest surviving testimony
to the human cost of divine purpose—
the lament of a man who mistook his gift for his god
and found salvation only in surrender.

When I finished transcribing the final leaf,
I understood why the seal read *"Zorah remembers."*
It was not a boast of lineage or pride of nation,
but a warning whispered to all who would inherit power.

May you read these words not as relic,
but as reflection.
For the pillars still stand,
and every generation must choose
whether to uphold them—or let them fall.

—*Dennis Logan,*
The Honorable Scribe,
Richmond, Virginia
Anno Domini 2025

Chapter I
The Cup of Dust

The Scribe's Preface, written in the prison house of Gaza

I came at dawn with a clay cup and a roll of skins.
The guards were drowsing, the flies awake.
Chains spoke softly where tongues were cruel.

Samson sat where the light could not reach.
Blind, yet listening as if the stones could answer.
His hair, shorn once, was a winter field returning.

"Brother," I said, "I have brought water."
He lifted his hands like a man tasting rain.
He drank slowly, as if each swallow were a prayer.

"Write," he told me, and I obeyed.
For I have known him since Zorah,
and I was taught letters while he was taught thunder.

The floor was grit and salt.
My reed was trembling in my hand.
I feared my script would waver like reed in wind.

Samson said:

"Begin where the covenant began, not where my locks were cut.
Men make relics of the hair,
but the vow is the root that lives beneath the skin.

My mother's whisper and my father's silence—
both were altars to the same Name.
I was girded in abstinence as in armor.

Strength is a lent fire.
We mistake the spark for the forge.
We kiss the ember and forget the mountain."

I set the reed, paused, and he heard the pause.
"Write the pause," he said, "for it speaks as well.
What is not said is the hinge of what is spoken."

He turned his face toward the cup I held.
"The taste of dust—write that also.
It keeps a man from worshiping his own thirst."

So I wrote the taste of dust.

We sat awhile with the flies and the breath of iron.
You could hear the millstones laboring in the yard,
and men hooting like children around a wounded lion.

"Delilah," he said then, quietly—
and the name was not a knife, but a bell.
Its peal crossed the room and died in the fetters.

"Write: I loved a voice that braided comfort with inquiry.
I thought curiosity was care.
I thought persistence was devotion.

She asked me where my strength lay, softly at first,
like rain mapping a hill it intends to move.
She smiled as one who measures while she sings.

I gave her riddles in circles.
I made a theater of my silence.
But pride is a sieve; all secrets pass it.

She did not slay me with steel, but with comfort.
Write that twice, scribe of Zorah.
She did not slay me with steel, but with comfort."

I wrote it twice, and beneath it I drew a small line,
for in our custom a small line is a memorial.
It binds the sentence to the conscience that hears it.

He sank back and breathed like a bellows spent.
Then he spoke as if lecturing his younger self:
"Beware the hand that dries your tears to count them.

Beware the lap that bargains with your sleep.
Love listens to keep; bribery listens to spend.
And a man hungry for praise will sell his future for echo."

He groped for the pillar behind him, found its pitted face.
"Do you remember," he asked me, "the day we ran the vineyards?
Your feet were books, my feet were birds."

"I remember," I said, and my voice was smaller than a boy's.
The reed scratched the skin like a cricket in dry grass.
I thought of boyhood, of figs warm with noon.

"Strength makes noise," he said. "Covenant makes silence.
I learned the noise first and made a god of it.
I came late to the silence and it undid me to mercy.

Write: the darkness I fear now is honest.
The light I wore before was full of mirrors.
I loved the mirror that loved me back."

He lifted his face, unseeing, and smiled without teeth.
"It is a mercy to lose the face that tempted you.
It is a mercy to be led like a child by a child."

From the court came the scrape of carts, the brag of guards.
The sun moved and did not enter.
I dipped the reed again, and ink bled like a wound.

"Tell me," I said, "how you walked toward the shears."
He nodded as if I had asked for fire in winter.
"A man follows his name to the cliff that fits it."

He continued:

"First came the laughter—hers like water, mine like bronze.
Bronze believes it sings; water knows it carves.
I was carved and called it being adored.

Then came the bargains—sleep for a secret,
kisses counted like coins,
questions folded in linen and set under my head.

Each answer I gave was a prayer to myself.
I wanted to be read like a psalm and kissed like a king.
A man in love with his legend is easy to rob."

He bowed his head.
The cup in my hand had cooled to the temperature of stone.
I thought of wells, and of the law that forbids idols of the heart.

"Write: the shears were no more terrible than a lullaby.
I slept in a hired tenderness.
I woke in a rented night."

His hands closed and opened, closed and opened.
I do not know if it was memory or a phantom pain.
The wrists remembered ropes the way a mouth remembers names.

"And afterward?" I asked, though the word bled shame.
He turned the sockets of his eyes toward the sound of my breath.
"Afterward I saw truly," he said, and almost laughed.

"They took my sight and gave me vision.
The darkness was not a tomb but a room without idols.
In it I learned the taste of the Name again."

We were silent then.
The chains eased as he leaned into the pillar.
I counted twelve heartbeats and set them in the margin.

He resumed in a softer register:

"Write for the young, scribe.
Write for the strong who have not yet been humbled.
Write for the humbled who think they have no more purpose.

Secrets kept from God will be bought by enemies.
The gift you parade will be priced by merchants.
Guard the covenant; the hair will take care of itself.

Let them know: desire is a river with two mouths—
one empties into union, the other into purchase.
I drank of both and called them the same."

He touched the ground with his palm, as if signing.
The dust clung to the scar as pollen to a bee.
He smiled the way a man does when he finally names his wound.

"The Lord is not undone by my undoing," he said.
"The vow outlives the violator.
Even now I am threaded to the Purpose."

I wrote that too, and made a second small line,
for such lines are bridges over memory's flood.
I mean for you, reader of ages, to cross them dry-footed.

"Do they taunt you still?" I asked, foolishly.
"They do," he answered, gentle as the wheel of night.
"But mockery is a flute; it cannot topple mountains."

He leaned forward, and the chain answered with its iron gospel.
"Bring me again tomorrow when the sun is loud.
Bring water, and the reed, and your patient ear.

For I must tell you how mercy keeps company with revenge,
and how a man can die without wasting his death.
There is counsel in the ruin; there is God in the ash."

He reached with both hands and found my wrist.
The grip was weaker than the lion's, stronger than my fear.
"Write this last for today," he said, and breathed:

"Strength is not what I lift, but what I lay down.
Glory is not what I keep, but what I return.
I am not finished, only unarmed."

I closed the skins and sealed them with twine.
The cup lay empty like a bitten moon.
The guards laughed; we did not.

When I rose, the air changed—
as if a door had turned on the other side of the world.
I could not say where, but I heard the future move.

This is the first account I, a son of Zorah, have written.
Let it be preserved among the laments and the laws,
that the young may learn the difference between hair and covenant.

And let the elders teach the proverb that follows:
Trust is the bread of vows; do not sell it for sweetness.
Comfort is a blade when it bargains with your soul.

So ends the first cup: dust, water, and warning.
Tomorrow I will return with ink and a listening heart.
For he has said there is counsel in the ruin, and I believe him.

Chapter II
The Whisper of Delilah

Written on the second day, in the prison house of Gaza.

I returned as the dawn cracked its jar of flame over the sea.
The guards mocked my persistence, saying,
"What gospel can a blind fool preach?"
I gave them bread and silence, and they let me pass.

Samson was awake, tracing the air as though it were a map.
The chains whispered with each gesture—
their links like the punctuation of his thought.

He said, "You have come back, as I asked."
"I have," I answered, unrolling the skin.
"Then write. Today I speak of her voice."

He began without prompt, his tone half prayer, half curse.

"Delilah was not the first to smile at my strength.
Others praised the lion I slew, the gates I tore from the city.
But she alone praised the boy who carried honey in his hands.
Do you understand? It is not flattery that fells a man,
but tenderness that pretends to see his soul."

He paused, listening for something beyond the walls.
"When she spoke, my rage forgot its name.
She asked what no one had dared:
Who are you without your might?
That question was a blade wrapped in silk.
I mistook the cut for caress."

I wrote that line twice, for he bade me:
"She asked what no one had dared.
Who are you without your might?"

He smiled faintly, remembering.

"She listened as if each word I said
was a lamp lit in her chest.
She wept when I spoke of loneliness—
and I thought, 'At last, one who mourns with me.'
But her tears were coins, scribe,
and she bought my trust with each one."

The air in the cell thickened with his grief.
Outside, a cart rolled over gravel, like distant thunder.

"Love is a covenant of mirrors," he continued.
"If both see the same reflection, the image endures.
But when one mirror hides behind smoke,
the other gazes into its own delusion."

He reached for the pillar, his fingers trembling.
"She asked again and again,
and each time I resisted,
the Lord withdrew a little more of His patience.
For I was proud of resisting.
I wore restraint as vanity."

He drew a slow breath.

"I thought my silence protected the vow.
But silence can become a monument to pride.
So I told her a fragment, a parable, a half-truth.
And she tested it with the laughter of her people.
Three times I deceived her.
Three times she returned, unbroken.

Her persistence was worship disguised as inquiry.
What god could resist worship?"

He laughed then—a sound like dry reeds burning.
"On the fourth, I grew weary of games.
She lay her head upon my chest and said,
'You speak in riddles because you are afraid to be known.'
And I—fool, prophet, victim—believed her."

He fell silent long enough that I thought him asleep.
When he spoke again, it was scarcely above a whisper.

"She sang me to sleep with a psalm that was not of Israel.
A song of rivers and men undone by their reflection.
When I woke, the covenant had fled,
and my eyes—those treacherous gates—were open no more."

He turned his sightless gaze toward me.
"Write: she did not betray me; I delivered myself to curiosity.
Write: she only opened the door I had built.
Write: the Lord allowed it, for I had worshiped my own gift."

I obeyed.

He sighed and drew his knees beneath him like a penitent.

"The seducer is not always wicked, scribe.
Sometimes she is sent as a teacher,
that the proud may be instructed through loss.
If I had been faithful to the silence of my vow,
I would have been deaf to her voice.
But my vanity needed an echo, and so I found her.
Every man summons his own Delilah
the moment he believes himself invincible."

The words fell heavy, like stones laid for an altar.

He asked for water, and I gave it.
As he drank, a fly landed upon his knuckle,
and he did not brush it away.
"I envy even the smallest creature," he said.
"It moves freely upon the earth.
But I am bound until I learn why the Lord allows chains."

I asked, "Do you hate her still?"

He shook his head.
"Hate is a luxury for those who still dream of justice.
I seek only meaning now.
The pillars will teach it to me."

When he spoke that word—*pillars*—
his whole frame seemed to remember its purpose.
The air trembled as if with unseen thunder.

"Write this for the generations to come:
The heart that hides its gift in another's hands
will wake one morning to find both empty.
Trust is the true Nazarite vow.
When it is broken, the temple begins to crack."

He leaned forward until the chain drew blood.
"Tomorrow, I will tell you what the Lord spoke
in the night of my blindness.
Then you will understand why the pillars still stand."

I closed the roll, sealing the ink with ash.
As I turned to leave, he said softly:
"Do not pity me, scribe. Pity the man
who has never been deceived—
for he has never been known."

And the chains sighed,
as though the earth itself mourned the sound of wisdom bound.

Chapter III
The Blinding

Written on the third day, in the prison house of Gaza.

The morning was dim, as if the sun itself were reluctant
to see what men had done.
The guards were gone to sport;
their laughter echoed down the corridor like a distant execution.
I entered quietly,
with oil for the lamp and the skin of yesterday's words.
Samson was awake, facing the wall. His head bowed low,
but his spine was a pillar yet unbroken.

When he heard my step, he said,
"So the world still turns, though I cannot see it."
I replied, "It turns more slowly, I think, when the mighty fall."
He smiled, thin as twilight.
"Or perhaps it turns faster, eager to be rid of us."

He lifted his face toward the dim glow.
"Sit, and write. Today I speak of the gift I mistook for glory,
and the blindness that opened my eyes."

He began with a whisper that grew as it went,
as if each word weighed more than his breath could bear.

"On the day they took my sight, I heard no cries of heaven.
No thunder, no lament.
Only the steady grind of the mill and the low chant of my enemies.
Their laughter was a song I had written with my own pride.
And the Lord was silent — not absent, but waiting."

He turned his palms upward, as if feeling rain that would not fall.
"I had been strong enough to lift gates and tear lions,

yet not strong enough to lift my heart from the mirror.
I had eyes for conquest, not compassion.
Now I have sockets for wisdom."

I paused, and he heard the pause.
"Write that slowly," he said.
"I have sockets for wisdom.
The eyes were lanterns, but their oil was arrogance."

He motioned to the pillar beside him and touched its surface,
fingers tracing cracks like a blind man reading scripture.
"These stones have watched men build gods and prisons alike.
I have lived long enough to learn they are the same.
A temple is but a cage men call holy,
and a cage but a temple that forgot how to pray."

He leaned closer.
"I see now that the Lord blinds those He loves most.
Not as punishment, but as purification.
Sight deceives. It measures. It desires.
But in darkness, you begin to hear the shape of things.
You begin to touch the presence hidden beneath the noise."

He bowed his head, and his tone softened.

"When I was a boy, I asked my father why the Nazirites drank no
wine.
He said, 'Because joy must remain unbought.'
But I learned to buy joy in the arms of women, in the praise of men,
in the weight of my own fame.
I made idols from applause.
And when the shears cut, I heard God's mercy in their blades."

He turned toward me then.
"You still have your eyes, scribe.
Do not trust them.
They will show you the world, but not your heart."

I nodded though he could not see.
"I will remember," I said.
"Write instead," he replied. "Remembering fades. Ink does not."

He spoke again after a long silence.
"I dream often of Delilah's hands — not their betrayal,
but their gentleness, how they soothed the very man they ruined.
I have forgiven her, but I have not forgiven myself.
I prayed once that the Lord would return my strength;
now I pray only that He return my purpose."

He clenched the chains and they rattled like wind in dry reeds.
"Strength is easy. Purpose is costly.
And those who mistake one for the other destroy both."

He gestured toward the sky he could not see.
"I was chosen to defend, not to dazzle.
But the people loved the dazzle, and so did I.
We are all mirrors of each other's vanity.
Now the mirror is gone, and only the face remains."

He turned his head slightly,
as though listening to something within.
"Last night the Lord spoke to me in the hush between dreams.
He said, 'You are not abandoned, only humbled.
The covenant is not broken — it is being rewritten in shadow.'
And I knew then that the hair was not my strength.
It was the memory of my vow returning.
It grows now not upon my head, but upon my spirit."

His mouth quivered between grief and laughter.
"I asked the Lord, 'Will You use me again?'
He answered, 'Yes, but not as before.
Your hands will destroy that which once celebrated you.'
And I wept until dawn,
for I saw that vengeance was but the shadow of justice,
and that both serve the same sun."

I set down the reed, but he continued speaking,
his words flowing like oil poured over stone.

"I have no sight, yet I see her face in every whisper.
I have no freedom, yet I feel the pillars tremble at my breath.
I have no future, yet I hear it approaching.
It walks in the voice of God calling me once more to obedience."

He leaned toward me,
close enough that I smelled the iron and sweat upon him.
"Write this, scribe, as the truth of all men who fall:
You cannot lose your purpose, only trade it.
And when you trade it for pleasure,
the Lord will buy it back with pain."

He laughed faintly then —
not the laugh of mockery, but of one who has finally understood.
"Tomorrow," he said, "I will tell you what I plan.
And when you write it, seal it with prayer, not pity."

When I left, the air behind me felt heavier.
The guards jeered, but their voices seemed far away.
I walked into the light and it felt dimmer than his darkness.

And I thought:
Perhaps blindness is not the absence of sight,
but the beginning of true vision.

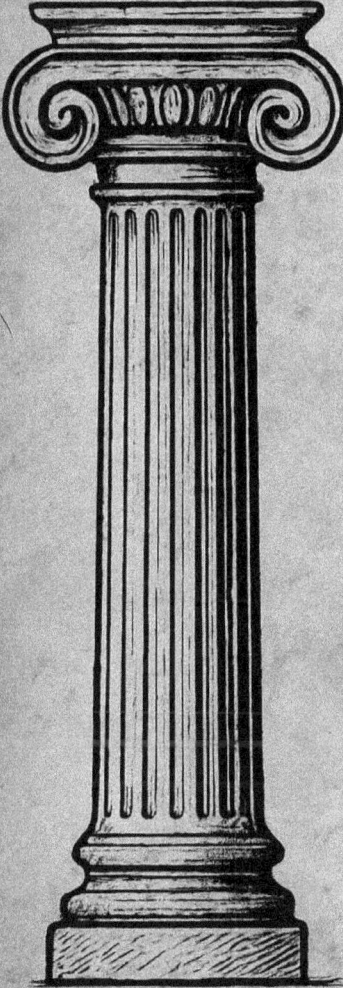

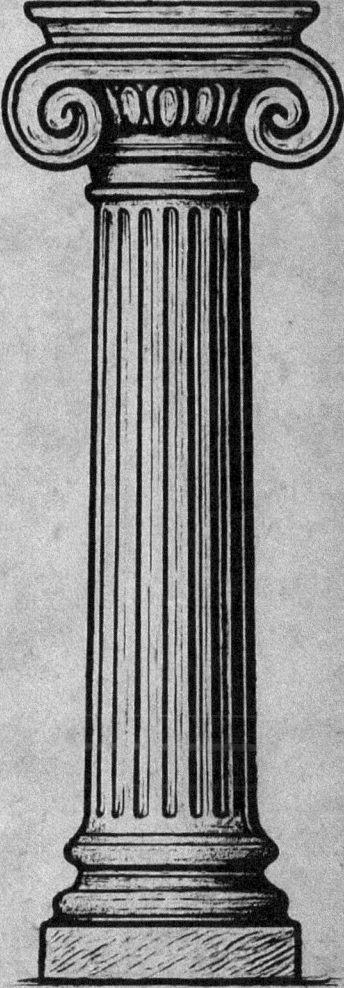

Chapter IV
The Covenant Renewed

Written on the fourth day, in the prison house of Gaza.

When I entered this morning, the air had changed.
The cell no longer felt like a tomb, but like a forge.
The guards muttered that the Nazarite
had begun to sing in the night.
They feared him again — not his strength, but his calm.
The peace of a man who has made covenant with ruin.

He sat upright, his hair grown wild and coiling
like roots reclaiming the earth.
His hands were steady. His voice, when he spoke,
carried the weight of thunder wrapped in prayer.

"Write," he said. "Today I speak of mercy and retribution,
and how the two are brothers in the house of the Lord."

He drew a deep breath and began:

"The covenant is not a promise one keeps for God.
It is the way God keeps Himself within a man.
I thought it a leash once —
a chain meant to bind my joy.
But now I see it as the breath that sustains me in exile.

I broke it when I desired to be adored.
And yet even in the breaking, it remembered me.
Covenant does not die when disobeyed;
it waits, patient as a seed under frost."

He lifted a hand toward the faint shaft of light.
"The hair grows again, yes — but so too the vow beneath it.

My strength returns not to avenge the past,
but to fulfill what pride interrupted."

He turned toward me, though his eyes were white as milk.
"The Lord whispered to me in darkness:
'What was cut shall rise.
But your revenge must serve redemption,
or it will turn you into what you hate.'

So I asked Him, 'Shall I not punish the Philistines for my eyes?'
And He said, 'Punish not for blindness,
but for the blindness they worship.'

Then I knew my purpose:
to pull down the house built upon arrogance,
to make of my death a sermon none could silence."

He paused. I could hear his heartbeat echo through the chains.
He was not trembling — he was remembering.

"Write this," he said softly.
"Mercy is not weakness.
It is the courage to suffer for meaning.
Retribution is mercy's shadow.
It follows close, not out of hatred, but out of justice.
And in the end, both are gathered into God."

He bowed his head as if before an altar.
"Do you see, scribe? The Lord did not take my strength.
He hid it until I learned how to wield it without pride."

He smiled faintly.
"When I was blind to humility, my might was a plague.
Now that I see, even in darkness,
my hands are temples of obedience.

I no longer ask to live — I ask to be used.
For a tool has no grief for its breaking
if the Maker's purpose is fulfilled."

He gestured toward the pillar beside him.
"These stones will learn His mercy through my death.
For when they fall, they will free a people from their idols,
and return glory to the One whose strength I borrowed."

His voice changed, lower now,
carrying an almost tender authority.

"I have dreamed of the temple of Dagon,
its walls trembling like reeds before the wind.
The people gather to mock me,
to dance upon the grave they have not yet dug.
They think the Lord has left me.
But He is already beneath their feet,
waiting in the dust for me to call His name."

He gripped the chain, his knuckles white as bone.
"Tomorrow, they will bring me there.
They think it a jest, a spectacle.
But they will witness the covenant renewed in thunder.
For I will stand between the pillars,
and cry not for vengeance, but for completion."

He fell silent for a time,
and when he spoke again, his words were almost a whisper.

"Write this for those who will read beyond my death:
God hides His greatest purposes in the ruins of our pride.
He builds temples from the ashes of our folly.
He blinds to restore sight,
and humbles to raise a voice that cannot be silenced."

Then he reached for my hand.
His fingers were warm, alive with a strange stillness.

"Tell them, my brother," he said,
"that strength without covenant is chaos,
and covenant without strength is slumber.
Only when both are joined does a man become the will of God."

He released me and lifted his face toward the faint light.
"Tomorrow will be my Sabbath, my rest.
And I will rest not in the grave,
but in the breath of the One who chose me."

I could not speak.
The air trembled with something unseen —
a holiness mingled with dread.

When I left, the guards asked why I wept.
I told them it was the dust,
but in truth, I wept because I had seen resurrection
before death had claimed its right.

And as I sealed the scroll,
I wrote this line beneath it:

*The covenant returns to those who have nothing left to offer but
themselves.*

Chapter V
The Pillars

The Final Testimony of the Scribe of Zorah

I was summoned by the guards at midmorning.
They said the lords of the Philistines desired sport—
and that the blind lion would dance for them.
I followed in silence, the roll of his words bound to my chest.
The dust of Gaza clung to my feet as if
it too were waiting to see what would come.

Samson walked between them,
guided by a boy no older than my own son.
Chains about his wrists, hair wild as a stormcloud,
he moved with a calm that frightened even his captors.
There was no struggle, only inevitability.
He walked like a man who had seen the script of his death
and found in it the handwriting of God.

The temple of Dagon was vast—
its roof upheld by two pillars of black stone,
its walls heavy with carvings of the sea god's triumphs.
Drums echoed like a heartbeat too large for the earth.
Thousands gathered on the balcony above,
their laughter like birds feasting on carrion.

When they saw Samson, they roared:
"Where is the strength of Israel now?
Where is the boast of your God?"
He did not answer.
He bowed his head,
and the boy led him forward by the hand.

I followed at a distance, unnoticed among the servants.
The child guided him to the center,
to where the pillars stood—
twin spines of stone reaching into the mouth of heaven.
Samson spoke softly to the boy,
and I crept close enough to hear.

"Place my hands upon the pillars that I may rest," he said.
"I am weary."
The boy obeyed,
not knowing he had placed destiny in motion.

Samson spread his palms upon the stone
and breathed as one who feels the pulse of the earth.
He whispered a prayer so low
I caught only fragments:

"O Lord, remember me once more...
Not for my pride, nor my vengeance...
But that they may know You still speak through the broken."

The crowd laughed again,
but the laughter faltered when they saw his head rise.
His lips moved,
and though his words were lost beneath the drums,
I felt them strike my chest like the beating of wings.

His voice rose above the noise—
not loud, but commanding,
as though the air itself had remembered who made it.

"Let me die with the Philistines," he cried,
"but let my death speak of covenant renewed!"

He bent his arms,
and the chains strained as if they too wished to flee.
The pillars groaned.

The floor beneath us shivered.
A silence fell—
the kind that comes before the thunder learns its name.

Then came the sound—
a deep cry, half human, half divine—
and the stone split.
The pillars cracked like ribs of an old god,
and the roof began to fold inward like a collapsing heaven.
The laughter became screams.
Dust rose like incense.
I fell to my knees,
shielding the scrolls with my body as the world broke open.

Through the chaos I heard Samson's voice once more,
not in pain, but in triumph:

"The Lord of Israel is not mocked!"

And then the thunder swallowed him.

When I awoke, there was light where the roof had been.
Smoke rose from the ruins like prayer escaping the throat of death.
Men and women lay in heaps among the shattered idols.
Samson's body was buried beneath the stones,
his arms still outstretched,
the pillars broken between them—
a cross of his own making.

I crawled to him and touched his hand.
It was still warm.
The boy who had led him stood nearby, weeping.
He asked, "Was this justice?"
And I said, "It was obedience."

I gathered the scrolls and wrote the final words upon the torn skin:

"He who blinded himself to the world
saw God clearly in the darkness.
His strength became his sacrifice,
and his death a covenant fulfilled."

I sealed them with the dust of Gaza,
and carried them back toward the hills of Zorah,
where his father still mourned in the fields.

There we buried him beside his mother,
and upon his stone I carved the words he left for the generations:

**Strength is not what we keep,
but what we return.
The covenant waits in the ruins of our pride.**

And thus ends the Testament of Samson—
the blind judge who saw too late,
the fallen hero who rose through ruin,
the man whose final breath turned vengeance into deliverance.

Epilogue:
The Scribe's Testament

Written many years after the fall of Gaza.

The years have rolled over me like waves over a stone,
smoothing the edges but never erasing the memory.
I am old now. My hands tremble when I unroll these skins,
but they still remember the rhythm of his voice.
Each line I wrote in the prison house of Gaza
still burns as if inked with fire rather than reed and soot.

I have seen kingdoms rise and call themselves eternal.
I have seen judges become tyrants and priests become merchants.
And in each, I have heard the echo of Samson's fall—
the sound of men who mistake their gifts for their gods.

When I think of him now, I no longer see the giant who tore lions
or the blind captive bound in chains.
I see the man who spoke softly to a boy and said,
"Let me rest my hands upon the pillars."
That moment was his true miracle.
He had found peace not in triumph,
but in surrender that fulfilled its purpose.

The world calls him destroyer.
I call him restorer.
For in tearing down the house of false worship,
he rebuilt the altar within himself.
He showed that covenant is not upheld by victory,
but by returning what was given—
even life itself—back into the hands of the Giver.

I once believed that blindness was punishment,
but time has taught me otherwise.
Those who see too clearly are seldom humble.
Those who walk in shadow learn to listen.
The Lord whispers most clearly to those
who have no illusions left to protect.

And what of Delilah?
History remembers her as seductress and betrayer.
Yet I have come to see her as mirror—
the reflection of what every man must face:
the power that flatters, the comfort that corrodes,
the hand that tests whether our love of God
is greater than our love of being adored.

She played her part as the whetstone of his faith.
Without her, Samson would have remained
a beast of strength, not a man of revelation.
She was the instrument of his undoing—
and thus, the midwife of his redemption.

These truths I have written not for scholars,
but for those who walk between pride and despair.
For every soul has its Delilah,
and every nation its temple of Dagon.
Each must choose whether to pull the pillars or bow before them.

The Lord hides His lessons in paradox:
that defeat is the seed of deliverance,
that blindness can teach vision,
that death, freely offered, outlasts the sword.

Samson learned this too late for himself,
but not too late for us.
Through his ruin we were shown that strength
is not measured in what endures,
but in what is willingly surrendered for truth.

I write these final words upon my last skin.
When I am gone, let this record be found
by those who seek not heroes, but meaning.

For the pillars still stand—in hearts, in empires, in idols.
And the Spirit still seeks hands willing to push.

**Blessed is the one who topples vanity in himself,
for he shall see the covenant renewed in his ruin.**

Afterword

It was September of 2023 when the tree fell.
A dead oak, hollow and waiting,
older than my house and heavier than sense.
I was in the studio shed that afternoon, recording Samson's story—
his final prayer, his blindness, the trembling of the pillars.
I had built that booth with my own hands,
each panel measured by faith and exhaustion.
It had become my temple of sound—
a place where the Word passed through flesh and into permanence.

I remember sitting on the futon,
the same old couch where I'd steal brief naps between sessions.
The air was still, the monitors silent.
I was debating whether to rest or record another passage.
And then—quietly, almost playfully—
a thought crossed my mind: *Not yet.*
It wasn't fear, not even caution—just a whisper of knowing.
So I stayed seated,
looking out the window at nothing in particular.

Moments later the world split open.

The sound was a kind of thunder that doesn't come from clouds.
A crack, a rush, a groan from the bones of the earth.
The oak beside my studio sheared in half,
collapsing through the roof,
ripping the room clean down the middle.
It crushed the booth I'd been recording in not ten minutes before,
the same booth that had carried the voice of Samson
only an hour earlier.
Had I chosen to nap,
had I lain back on that futon instead of sitting up,
I would not be writing this now.

I watched the studio I built split like scripture—
a divine line through plywood and prophecy.
My microphone lay buried beneath insulation and splinters,
the headphones still wrapped around the Bible open on the stand.
For a long while I didn't move.
I just listened to the ringing silence,
the echo of what *almost was.*

That night I sat outside, staring at the wreckage by flashlight.
The booth was demolished completely,
but somehow the futon—my seat—remained untouched.
The irony wasn't lost on me:
Samson had pulled pillars; I had been spared by one.
He died when the walls fell;
I was given another chance to finish the work.

Was it coincidence?
Intuition?
Divine interruption?
I still don't know.
Sometimes I think I slipped timelines that day—
that I was crushed in one and woke up in another.
Other times I believe I was simply reminded
that purpose, once chosen, doesn't release you so easily.

Either way, something was rewritten in me.

People ask if I carry trauma from it.
I don't know how to answer.
When you have children,
when you're building, feeding, recording, repairing—
you don't have the luxury of unraveling.
You just keep going.
Maybe that's courage, maybe it's duty.
Maybe it's just love disguised as stubbornness.

I rebuilt the shed in pieces.
Some nights I'd sweep until midnight,
others I'd sit on that same futon,
staring at the gap in the roof where light now fell clean and pure.
By May of 2025, *The Universal Bible* was finished.
One hundred twenty-five hours of voice,
recorded between the collapse and the completion.

Now, every time I hear Samson's story,
I hear not the sound of his death,
but the echo of that tree falling beside me.
He prayed to be used one last time;
I was spared to keep being used.
He pushed the pillars; I watched mine fall and rise again.

I don't claim to know what saved me—
angel, instinct, or the whisper of an unseen scribe.
But I know the timing was holy.
I know the booth I built became the sermon I needed to hear:
that everything we make is temporary,
but the act of making is eternal.

The tree fell to my right.
The booth was demolished.
I remained—unfinished, unbroken, unburied.

And that is why I write.
Why I record.
Why I call myself The Honorable Scribe.
Because once you've heard your own story
echoed in the fall of a tree,
you understand that every word afterward is resurrection.

On the Covenant of Falling and Finishing

In every age, the story repeats itself.
A man builds, and what he builds is struck down.
A voice rises, and what it speaks costs the breath that made it.
The pillar, the booth, the body—each is a temple for a time,
and each must fall for the covenant to be renewed.

When I first read the *Testament of Samson*,
I thought it was a tale of vengeance.
But after the tree fell beside me—splitting the studio in two,
destroying the booth I'd built to house my voice—
I came to understand it differently.
It was never about destruction.
It was about completion.

Samson did not die for rage; he died for release.
He fulfilled what his strength had delayed.
In his ruin, the purpose he'd resisted was finally revealed.
And in that, I recognized something of myself.

When the oak came down, it erased months of my labor—
but it also erased my illusion of control.
It reminded me that the structure is never the sacred thing;
it is only the vessel for a moment of obedience.
I had built walls to capture the Word,
but it took the fall of those walls to remind me
that the Word was already free.

The parallels still haunt me:
Samson between the pillars, arms outstretched;
me sitting on that futon, the booth collapsing beside me.
Both of us surrounded by what we had built,
both hearing a whisper that said, *This is not the end.*
He gave his life to finish his story.
I was given mine back to finish the same.

I've come to believe that covenant is not a contract with heaven;
it is the echo that follows obedience.
Every time we choose to continue—
to rebuild, to record,
to raise our children, to finish what we start—
we renew that echo.
We become, in our small ways,
the living continuation of ancient vows.

That is why this *Testament of Samson* matters.
Not as archaeology, not as legend, but as mirror.
For every artist, every parent, every believer or skeptic—
the pillars still stand in us: pride and despair,
strength and surrender.
Each of us will be asked, one day, to choose which to push.

I do not think the tree fell *at* me; I think it fell *for* me.
To remind me that work is sacred, but not eternal.
To remind me that my voice was never trapped in a booth,
but carried in the breath that survived it.
Samson found his purpose in the fall.
I found mine beside it.

So I dedicate this recovered gospel,
and the voice that bears it,
to all who labor in silence—
those who build temples of wood, sound, or word,
and learn through collapse that nothing made by hands
is ever truly lost.

For every fall contains a call,
and every ruin remembers the craftsman who dared to build it.

—Dennis Logan
The Honorable Scribe
Richmond, Virginia
Anno Domini 2025

Also Hear These Works in the Voice of Dennis Logan

Over the past decade I have devoted thousands of hours to
recording sacred texts, apocrypha, and esoteric classics.
If *The Testament of Samson* spoke to you,
you can continue the journey through these and many more
audiobooks available on Audible and other platforms:

*Search "Dennis Logan" on Audible for the complete catalogue of
100+ works across scripture, history, spirituality, folklore,
mysticism, occultism, and esoteric literature.*

Scripture, Apocrypha & Ancient Texts

- *The Universal Bible* of the Protestant, Catholic,
  Orthodox, Ethiopic, Syriac, and Samaritan Church
- *Lost Books of the Bible: The Great Rejected Texts*
- *The Book of Jasher*
- Book of Enoch, Jubilees, Jasher & The Book of
  Giants: The Complete Scriptures of Nephilim &
  Fallen Angels
- The Books of Enoch and The Book of Giants (featuring
  1, 2, and 3 Enoch with the Aramaic and Manichean
  Giants texts)
- The Book of Jubilees: The Little Genesis, The
  Apocalypse of Moses
- *The First and Second Books of Adam and Eve*
- *The Kebra Nagast : The Glory of the Kings*
- The Book of the Bee: The Syriac Text
- The Holy Piby: The Blackman's Bible
- The Gospel of Barnabas

Gnostic, Mystical & Esoteric Studies

- *Banned from the Bible*
- *The Gnostic Gospels of Philip, Mary Magdalene, and Thomas*
- *The Gnostic Scriptures*
- *An Advanced Lesson in Gnosticism*
- The Secret Teachings of All Ages
- *The Kybalion, Tablet of Hermes & Emerald Tablets*
- *Thought-Forms*
- *The Initiates of the Flame*
- *The Way of Initiation*
- *Golden Verses of Pythagoras*
- *The Gateless Gate*
- Science of Breath

Magick & Occult Classics

- *The Book of the Sacred Magic of Abramelin the Mage*
- *The Lesser Key of Solomon*
- An Outline of Occult Science: A Modern Edition

Myth, Folklore & Religious Narratives

- *Legends of the Yoruba*
- *Aradia: The Gospel of the Witches*
- *The Wisdom of King Solomon*

Original Works by Dennis Logan

- *The Panerotic Sutras of Master Stryfe*
- *The Apocatastasis of Enoch*
- *The Testament of Samson*

`www.ingramcontent.com/pod-product-compliance
Lightning Source LLC
`rsburg PA
`735020426
`B00008B/2049